Title

# HIGH-OCTANE SUCCESS:

Mastering Time, Achieving Greatness, Transforming Into reality.

Sean,N.morias

## INTRODUCTION

In a society filled with infinite diversions, continual change, and ever-growing to-do lists, the thought of a year sometimes seems like a huge period, stretching out eternally before us. We make yearly objectives with the best of intentions, only to find ourselves scurrying to meet them as the year hurtles toward its inevitable finish.

But what if I told you that you could improve your life, your company, and your future in only 12 weeks?

Welcome to "The 12 Week Year," where we question the standard conception of a year and introduce you to a new concept that will transform your approach to goal-setting, productivity, and achievement. In this book, we will walk you through a strong framework that allows you to do more in 12 weeks than most people do in a full year.

Drawing from the fields of business, psychology, and personal development, "The 12 Week Year" presents a blueprint to break free from the cycle of procrastination and unrealized potential. It's a roadmap for leveraging the urgency of a 12-week time limit to produce substantial, enduring outcomes.

Whether you're an entrepreneur aiming to launch your company to new heights, a professional striving to flourish in your field, or an individual hoping to make fundamental personal changes, this book is your guide to accomplishing more with focused intensity, clarity, and purpose.

# CHAPTER 1

: THE FOUNDATION

In the opening chapter of our quest, "The Foundation," we construct the structure for what lies ahead. This essential chapter lays the foundation for the full tale, providing major people, themes, and the fundamental conflict that will define our trip.

As we dig into the lives of our characters and study the surroundings they inhabit, we begin to unearth the secrets and obstacles that will push the story forward. "The Foundation" is where the seeds of inquiry are sowed, and the reader is urged to go on a quest for knowledge, insight, and discovery.

This chapter serves as the cornerstone upon which the rest of the narrative will be erected. It not only shows the characters' reasons and aims but also hints at the problems they must confront to attain their goals. As you continue reading, pay an eye on the little nuances and foreshadowing within "The Foundation," since they will become crucial in the chapters to come.

With anticipation increasing and questions emerging, chapter 1 sets the setting for a compelling and thought-provoking journey that will unravel in the pages to come. Enjoy the adventure that lies ahead as we explore the depths of "The Foundation.

## • **DEFINING YOUR VISION AND VALUES**

1. Setting objectives is a vital step toward attaining success in both your personal and professional life. Here are some crucial elements to consider while creating your goals:

2. Clarity: Define your objectives with maximum clarity. Whether they be personal or professional, make sure you know precisely what you want to accomplish. Vague objectives are difficult to strive for.

3. Specificity: Instead of creating a generic aim like "be successful," break it down into particular, quantifiable targets. For example, in your working life, you can

strive towards a specific position, income, or project completion.

4. Realism: While it's fine to dream big, ensure that your objectives are practical and feasible. Setting unreasonable objectives may lead to anger and disappointment.

5. Timeframes: Establish a timeframe for your objectives. Having deadlines might inspire you to take consistent action.

6. Balance: Consider how your personal and professional objectives match with each other. Striking a balance is vital for general well-being.

7. Prioritization: Not all objectives are of equal value. Identify your main priorities and concentrate your efforts on them.

8. Measuring Progress: Regularly analyze your progress toward your objectives. This enables you to make modifications if required and celebrate your successes along the road.

9. Adaptability: Life is unpredictable, and circumstances change. Be open to revising your objectives as required to keep connected with your developing desires.

10. Resources and Support: Identify the resources and support systems necessary to assist you in reaching your objectives.

This might be education, mentors, or financial planning.

11. Persistence: Understand that reaching significant objectives frequently requires time and effort. Stay persistent, even in the face of failures.

12. Record-Keeping: Keep a record of your objectives and progress. This might help you keep organized and motivated.

13. Self-Care: Remember that your well-being is vital. Ensure that your objectives encourage a good work-life balance.

- **SETTING YOUR PERSONAL AND PROFESSIONAL GOALS**

1. Setting objectives is a vital step toward attaining success in both your personal

and professional life. Here are some crucial elements to consider while creating your goals:

2. Clarity: Define your objectives with maximum clarity. Whether they be personal or professional, make sure you know precisely what you want to accomplish. Vague objectives are difficult to strive for.

3. Specificity: Instead of creating a generic aim like "be successful," break it down into particular, quantifiable targets. towards example, in your working life, you can strive towards a specific position, income, or project completion.

4. Realism: While it's fine to dream big, ensure that your objectives are practical and feasible. Setting unreasonable objectives may lead to anger and disappointment.

5. Timeframes: Establish a timeframe for your objectives. Having deadlines might inspire you to take consistent action.

6. Balance: Consider how your personal and professional objectives match with each other. Striking a balance is vital for general well-being.

7. Prioritization: Not all objectives are of equal value. Identify your main priorities and concentrate your efforts on them.

8. Measuring Progress: Regularly analyze your progress toward your objectives. This enables you to make modifications if required and celebrate your successes along the road.

9. Adaptability: Life is unpredictable, and circumstances change. Be open to revising your objectives as required to keep connected with your developing desires.

10. Resources and Support: Identify the resources and support systems necessary to assist you reach your objectives. This might be education, mentors, or financial planning.

11. Persistence: Understand that reaching significant objectives frequently requires

time and effort. Stay persistent, even in the face of failures.

12. Record-Keeping: Keep a record of your objectives and progress. This might help you keep organized and motivated.

13. Self-Care: Remember that your well-being is vital. Ensure that your objectives encourage a good work-life balance.

# CHAPTER 2:

## THE 12-WEEK YEAR CYCLE

1. The 12-week Year Cycle is a potent productivity and goal-setting paradigm that condenses standard yearly objectives into shorter, more concentrated periods of 12 weeks. This strategy is aimed to promote responsibility, productivity, and agility in attaining goals. Here are some crucial aspects to consider:

2. Shorter Timeframes: Instead of defining annual objectives, the 12-week Year encourages you to define and prioritize your goals within a 12-week timeframe.

This tight timeframe generates a feeling of urgency and reduces procrastination.

3. Focus on Execution: The system stresses execution over preparation. It encourages people and organizations to break down bigger objectives into smaller, achievable tasks that may be accomplished within the 12-week cycle.

4. Regular Review: Frequent check-ins are necessary throughout the 12-week Year. Weekly evaluations and changes help you remain on track and make required course improvements to reach your goals.

5. Accountability: The framework fosters personal accountability and responsibility for goal attainment. Regular

accountability sessions with yourself or a mentor/team guarantee that you're continually working towards your objectives.

6. Flexibility: Unlike typical yearly planning, the 12-week Year enables you to alter your objectives and tactics more rapidly depending on changing circumstances or priorities.

7. Measurable Results: Setting specified, measurable, attainable, relevant, and time-bound (SMART) objectives is a vital part of this method. It ensures that your goals are clear and measurable.

8. Balanced Goals: The 12-week Year emphasizes a balanced approach to goal

planning, including several facets of life, such as employment, health, and personal growth.

9. Continuous Improvement: After each 12-week cycle, you have the chance to analyze your performance, learn from your experiences, and adjust your goal-setting process for the next cycle.

10. Motivation: The shorter timelines typically contribute to greater motivation and a feeling of achievement as you achieve and celebrate your objectives more regularly.

11. Adaptability: This technique is adaptable and may be used for personal objectives,

professional endeavors, or team activities. It's adaptable to numerous circumstances.

## • UNDERSTANDING THE QUARTERLY RHYTHM

The quarterly rhythm refers to the technique of structuring work, objectives, and projects into three-month periods. It's a helpful approach for corporations, teams, and people alike. Here's why it matters:

attention and Accountability: Breaking the year into quarters allows for enhanced attention on particular goals. It enables organizations and individuals to set clear, attainable objectives within a shorter period, boosting responsibility.

flexibility: In a continuously changing environment, quarterly regularity encourages flexibility. It helps us to examine and alter our plans and objectives every few months, ensuring we remain aligned with changing conditions and market dynamics.

Measurement and Evaluation: Quarterly cycles make it easy to monitor progress. Regular evaluations allow the opportunity to celebrate triumphs, highlight areas for improvement, and pivot if required.

Strategic Planning: Planning in quarterly cycles assists in long-term strategic planning. It ensures that short-term goals contribute to broader objectives and avoid becoming buried in day-to-day chores.

Motivation and Momentum: Achieving quarterly objectives creates a feeling of success and momentum. It keeps teams engaged and energetic throughout the year.

To make the most of the quarterly rhythm, consider the following:

Establish your objectives for each quarter.

Break down these objectives into practical tasks and assign responsibilities.

Regularly assess progress and make necessary modifications.

Celebrate triumphs and learn from failures.

Embracing the quarterly cycle may lead to better productivity, improved performance, and a more nimble approach to reaching success. It's a strong tool for people and organizations aiming for continual development and greatness.

I invite you to study how this notion might help your job and life. Feel free to contact out if you'd want to discuss it more.

- **BREAKING DOWN THE 12 WEEKS**

Embarking on a 12-week adventure is an exciting chance for development and success. This timeline gives a systematic way to reach your objectives, whether they are connected to health, personal growth, or a particular endeavor. To make the most of these 12 weeks, it's necessary to break down the trip into achievable segments. Here's a tutorial on how to accomplish precisely that:

Set Clear Goals: Begin by outlining what you want to accomplish in these 12 weeks. Be detailed, quantifiable, and practical in your goal-setting. Whether it's running a marathon, creating a company, or honing a talent, clarity is crucial.

Create a Roadmap: Outline the important milestones you need to attain during the 12 weeks. Divide your aim into smaller, attainable activities. This plan will act as your guide during the voyage.

Weekly Planning: Break your 12-week trip into weekly chunks. Each week should have a defined emphasis or aim. Plan what you need to accomplish each week to go closer to your objectives.

Daily Action: Translate your weekly plans into daily chores. What can you do each day to work toward your weekly goals?

These everyday acts are the building blocks of success.

Track development: Maintain a notebook or use a digital tool to track your development. This helps you keep responsible and enables you to make modifications if required.

Stay Flexible: Life may throw curveballs, so be prepared to alter your strategy as required. Flexibility is crucial to overcoming hurdles and keeping on course.

Seek Support: Share your objectives with friends, family, or a mentor. Their support and input may be priceless.

Celebrate Milestones: Acknowledge and appreciate your victories along the road. Recognizing your progress may enhance motivation.

Review and Adjust: Regularly examine how you're performing. Are you on schedule to accomplish your 12-week goal? If not, change your strategy and keep going ahead.

Stay Committed: Remember why you began this 12-week adventure in the first place. Stay devoted, even when the going gets difficult.

Learn and Grow: Embrace the learning opportunities that come with adversities. Every setback is an opportunity to learn and develop.

Finish Strong: As you near the conclusion of your 12 weeks, push yourself to finish strong. Reflect on how far you've come and utilize that momentum to cross the finish line.

Breaking down your 12 weeks into small chunks may convert what feels like a difficult trip into a doable one. remain focused, and remain motivated, and in 12 weeks, you'll be astounded at what you've done.

# CHAPTER 3:

WEEKLY EXECUTION

- I hope this communication finds you well. I wanted to present you with a snapshot of our weekly execution progress. Our team has been actively working on many initiatives, and I'm delighted to discuss our successes and next ambitions.
- Project Updates:
- Project A: We successfully finished the first phase of Project A, and we are presently in the testing and

optimization stage. We remain on schedule to reach our milestone by [date].

- Project B: This project is developing nicely, with the development phase approaching conclusion. We anticipate going into the testing phase next week.

- Project C: We experienced some unforeseen issues in Project C, which resulted to a slight delay. However, we have altered our timetable and are confident in a revised completion date.

- Key Achievements: We reached a big milestone in cutting

manufacturing costs by [%], resulting in enhanced profitability.

- o Our customer satisfaction rates continue to grow, indicating our dedication to offering high-quality products/services.

- o problems and Mitigation: We are aware of the problems created by [particular obstacles], and we have established a mitigation strategy to handle these concerns effectively.

- o next Goals: Our key objective for the next week is to assure the successful launch of Project A and to dedicate more resources to accelerate Project C.

- We will also continue to review key performance indicators (KPIs) to ensure that we are on pace to fulfill our quarterly objectives.

- Team teamwork: The teamwork and devotion of our team members have been important in our growth. I wish to offer my thanks to each member for their hard work and devotion.

- Open for Feedback:

- Your opinions and thoughts are incredibly helpful to us. Please feel free to submit any recommendations or problems you may have with our weekly

# • WEEKLY PLANNING

I wanted to offer some ideas on the art of mastering weekly planning, a  and general well-being. Effective weekly planning is a strong tool that may help you remain organized, prioritize chores, and make the most of your time.

Set Clear Goals: Begin by outlining your broad objectives, both short-term and long-term. Having a strong idea of what you want to accomplish helps drive your weekly planning process.

Prioritize Tasks: Identify the most critical assignments for the week. Consider deadlines, priority, and urgency. Focus on what genuinely matters.

Time Blocking: Allocate precise time windows for tasks and activities. This helps develop an organized timetable, lowering the risk of procrastinating.

Flexibility: While preparation is necessary, understand that life may be unexpected. Allow for some flexibility in your schedule to allow unforeseen occurrences or adjustments.

Break Tasks Down: Large undertakings may be daunting. Break things down into smaller, attainable stages to make success more feasible.

Use Tools: Utilize digital or physical tools like calendars, to-do lists, or project management software to keep track of your goals and chores.

examine and Reflect: After each week, examine what you achieved and what didn't go as planned. Use this reflection to enhance your plans.

Self-Care: Don't forget to plan time for self-care, relaxation, and things you like. Balancing work and personal life is vital for long-term success.

Delegate When Possible: If you have the opportunity, assign work to others to free up your time for more vital pursuits.

Consistency: Make weekly planning a regular habit. The more you practice, the better you'll get at maximizing your time and attaining your objectives.

Remember that weekly planning is a dynamic process. It's about establishing a rhythm that works best for you and modifying it as required. By learning this ability, you may boost your productivity, minimize stress, and make consistent progress toward your goals.

- **THE ROLE OF THE WEEKLY ROUTINE**

The weekly routine plays a vital role in our lives, offering structure, stability, and countless advantages. It acts as a cornerstone for productivity, personal development, and general well-being.

Firstly, a well-designed weekly routine helps us manage our time effectively. It lets us devote precise blocks of time to particular jobs and obligations, ensuring that nothing crucial gets missed. This time management component assists considerably in lowering stress and enhancing productivity.

Furthermore, a regular weekly regimen assists in building beneficial behaviors. When we repeat specific behaviors or goals often, they get engrained in our everyday lives, making it simpler to attain our aims. Whether it's exercise, studying, or spending quality time with loved ones, a weekly routine offers the structure for building these habits.

Additionally, the weekly schedule improves work-life balance. Assigning time for both work-related responsibilities and recreational activities, helps us establish a happy balance. This balance helps to enhance mental and emotional well-being, minimizing fatigue and generating a feeling of satisfaction.

Moreover, the weekly schedule fosters responsibility and goal attainment. When we create weekly objectives or tasks, we can monitor our progress more efficiently and alter our plans appropriately. This feeling of responsibility keeps us motivated and on track toward our long-term ambitions.

# CHAPTER 4:

## THE POWER OF DAILY ACTIONS

I wanted to share a thought with you on the enormous power of everyday deeds. It's frequently easy to underestimate the importance of tiny, regular efforts in our lives. Yet, it's these everyday activities that may lead to tremendous transformations and triumphs.

Think about it — the world's greatest accomplishments weren't completed in a single gigantic jump, but via innumerable everyday steps made towards a goal.

Whether it's personal development, job success, or a healthy lifestyle, the answer resides in the dedication to everyday activities.

Each day presents a chance to make progress, learn, and inch closer to our ambitions. It's a reminder that we don't need to wait for a perfect time or huge effort to get started. Instead, it's the cumulative impact of these modest, repeated activities that generates momentum and promotes enduring change.

So, let's embrace the power of everyday activities in our life. Set modest, manageable objectives, then take continuous steps toward them. Remember, it's not about the magnitude of the action but the tenacity in performing it day after day. Over time, you'll be astounded at what you can do.

Here's to the strength of everyday acts and the road towards our ambitions.

- **LEVERAGING DAILY EXECUTION**

I wanted to underline the necessity of leveraging everyday execution in our business and personal life. Daily execution isn't simply about going through the motions; it's about continuously and consciously progressing towards our objectives.

By concentrating on everyday execution, we develop a tremendous momentum that pulls us ahead. Here are a few crucial items to consider:

Consistency creates success: Success is frequently the consequence of little, everyday efforts performed over time. By completing our responsibilities regularly, we create habits that lead to accomplishment.

Adaptability: Daily execution enables us to adjust and pivot as required. We can monitor progress regularly and make modifications swiftly, ensuring we remain on the correct course.

Reducing overwhelm: Breaking huge ambitions into everyday chores makes them more achievable. This relieves tension and stops us from feeling overwhelmed by the vastness of our aims.

Continuous improvement: Daily execution encourages learning and progress. Each day gives a chance to perfect our abilities and approach, constantly enhancing our performance.

Achieving long-term objectives: When we regularly perform our everyday duties in harmony with our long-term goals, we inch closer to attaining those ambitions. It's the everyday grind that lays the basis for our aspirations.

Remember, everyday execution is about identifying priorities, remaining organized, and sustaining focus. It's not about accomplishing everything but doing the correct things consistently. Let's commit to use everyday execution as a great instrument for our personal and professional growth.

- **BUILDING CONSISTENCY AND MOMENTUM**

I wanted to underline the necessity of creating consistency and momentum in our undertakings. Consistency is the foundation upon which development is built, while momentum pulls us ahead towards our objectives.

Consistency requires establishing a commitment to frequent, purposeful acts. It's about turning up every day, even when the going gets rough. When we constantly put in the work, we build a rhythm that becomes a habit, making it simpler to remain on track.

Momentum, on the other hand, is the force that accelerates our journey. It's the product of our constant efforts throughout time. When we generate momentum, each stride ahead gets simpler, and we acquire confidence in our skills.

To develop consistency and momentum:

Set Clear Goals: Define what you intend to accomplish, both short-term and long-term. Having defined goals provides your efforts direction.

Create a Routine: Establish a daily or weekly regimen that matches your objectives. Consistency thrives on structure.

Stay Accountable: Share your objectives with someone who can keep you responsible. This might be a buddy, mentor, or coach.

Embrace Small Steps: Progress may appear gradual at first, but every tiny step adds to your momentum. Celebrate your victories along the road.

Learn from Setbacks: Don't let disappointments discourage you. Instead, embrace them as chances to learn and develop. Adjust your strategy and keep pushing ahead.

Focus on Discipline: Discipline is the bridge between consistency and momentum. It's the dedication to accomplishing what has to be done, even when motivation wanes.

Remember, creating consistency and momentum is a process that demands patience and devotion.

Over time, your efforts will compound, and you'll find yourself producing astonishing outcomes. Keep pushing ahead, and you'll achieve new heights of accomplishment.

# CHAPTER 5

: THE FOUR DISCIPLINES

"The Four Disciplines" is a strong framework for accomplishing corporate objectives and personal success, as defined in the book "The 4 Disciplines of Execution" by Stephen R. Covey, Chris McChesney, and Sean Covey. These disciplines are:

Focus on the Wildly Important: This profession stresses the necessity of identifying and prioritizing a limited number of key goals. By reducing your emphasis to a few core objectives, you can concentrate your energy and resources more efficiently.

Act on the Lead measurements: Instead of only focusing on lag measurements (results), this discipline stresses the identification and monitoring of lead measures. Lead measurements are predictive and may be modified directly. They give early signs of success or failure and permit course modifications.

Keep a Compelling Scoreboard: People are more motivated and engaged when they can see their progress. A captivating scoreboard is a visual depiction of your objectives and their current progress. It keeps everyone aligned and responsible.

Create a Cadence of Accountability: Regular meetings and check-ins are vital for ensuring that people and teams remain dedicated to their objectives. These workshops promote a feeling of ownership and duty, promoting a culture of accountability.

Implementing these disciplines helps businesses and people transform strategic purpose into quantifiable outcomes. By keeping focus, acting on lead measures, employing scoreboards, and creating responsibility, you may greatly increase your capacity to accomplish what matters most.

- **DISCIPLINE 1: VISION**

Vision is the basic discipline that drives people and organizations toward their intended future. It functions as a compass, offering direction, purpose, and drive. Here are essential aspects to consider:

Clarity of Purpose: A clear vision reveals the "why" behind your activities. It identifies your ultimate objectives and helps you grasp what you are working towards.

Inspiration: A captivating vision encourages people and teams to strive for excellence. It awakens passion and feeds resolve, making it easier to conquer hurdles.

Long-Term Focus: Vision supports long-term thought and planning. It helps you to look past present problems and remain dedicated to your objectives.

Alignment: For enterprises, a common vision aligns teams and stakeholders. It generates solidarity and a feeling of belonging, promoting cooperation and synergy.

Adaptability: While a vision offers guidance, it should also be adaptive. In a quickly changing environment, the capacity to alter the vision without surrendering essential principles is vital.

Communication: Effectively conveying your vision is vital. It should be clear, succinct, and readily understood by everyone concerned.

Measurement and Progress: Regularly analyze progress toward your objective. This entails defining goals, monitoring performance, and making required modifications.

In short, Discipline 1: Vision is about identifying your mission, motivating action, and creating a blueprint for achievement. It acts as a guiding light, helping people and organizations through the difficulties of life and work.

- **DISCIPLINE 2: PLANNING**

1. Planning is a crucial part of obtaining success and order in both personal and

professional undertakings. It is the disciplined activity of creating defined objectives, developing strategies, and coordinating resources to attain certain goals. Effective planning acts as a blueprint that directs our activities, reduces uncertainty, and increases productivity. Here are crucial elements to consider when it comes to Discipline 2: Planning:

2. Goal Setting: The basis of planning is establishing your objectives. Whether short-term or long-term, objectives give direction and purpose. They should be SMART (Specific, Measurable, Achievable, Relevant, and Time-bound) to be successful.

3. Strategic Thinking: Planning requires thinking strategically about how to reach your objectives. This typically requires breaking down enormous tasks into smaller, doable stages.

4. Resource Allocation: Identify the resources necessary to implement your

strategy, including time, money, staff, and supplies. Allocate them effectively to avoid waste.

5. dates: Establish specific dates and deadlines for each element of your strategy. This helps establish a feeling of urgency and responsibility.

6. Flexibility: While preparation is necessary, it's equally essential to be flexible. Be prepared to adapt your strategy when circumstances change or new information becomes available.

7. Risk Assessment: Evaluate possible risks and problems that may develop during the execution of your strategy. Develop contingency measures to reduce these hazards.

8. Monitoring and Evaluation: Continuously assess progress toward your objectives and make modifications as appropriate. Regularly review the efficacy of your strategy and be open to modifications.

9. Communication: Effective planning typically entails cooperation and

communication with others. Ensure that all stakeholders are informed and aligned with the plan's goals.

10. Personal Planning: Planning is not restricted to work or projects. It's equally vital for personal growth. Set objectives for self-improvement, health, and well-being, and plan how to attain them.

- **DISCIPLINE 3: PROCESS CONTROL**

1. In the field of organizational management and efficiency, Discipline 3: Process Control plays a vital role in ensuring that activities function smoothly and consistently. This profession comprises the methodical management of processes to meet stated goals, maintain quality standards, and adapt to changing

situations. Here are some crucial factors to consider while handling Discipline 3: Process Control:

2. Process Definition and Documentation: The first step in successful process control is to fully identify and record all important processes inside your business. This involves describing the exact tasks, responsibilities, and sequence of actions involved.

3. uniformity: Once procedures are developed, uniformity is crucial. Establishing regular methods helps limit differences in production, decreases mistakes, and promotes overall efficiency.

4. Performance Metrics: Metrics and key performance indicators (KPIs) should be defined to monitor the efficacy and efficiency of processes. Regularly monitoring these indicators provides for prompt detection of discrepancies and areas in need of improvement.

5. Feedback Loops: Implementing feedback loops is critical for process control. Feedback methods enable ongoing monitoring and modification, ensuring that processes stay aligned with company objectives and consumer expectations.

6. Quality Assurance: Ensuring the quality of goods or services is a vital part of process control. Implement quality control

procedures to identify errors and maintain high standards throughout the manufacturing or service delivery process.

7. Adaptability: While uniformity is vital, procedures must also be responsive to changing situations. A well-designed process control framework should allow for alterations in reaction to market movements or internal changes.

8. Automation and Technology: Embracing technology and automation may expedite operations and boost control. Utilize software, tools, and data analytics to enhance decision-making and eliminate human error.

9. Risk Management: Identify possible hazards within processes and devise solutions to manage them. Effective process control entails planning for eventualities and reducing interruptions.

10. Continuous Improvement: Process control is a continual activity. Encourage a culture of continuous improvement where staff actively explore methods to better procedures and efficiency.

11. Training and Development: Invest in training and development programs to ensure that personnel understand and adhere to established practices. Well-trained teams are more likely to contribute to effective process control.

- **DISCIPLINE 4: SCOREKEEPING**

1. Scorekeeping is a crucial component of any undertaking, whether it be in sports, business, or personal growth. It serves as a basic tool for measuring progress, analyzing performance, and making informed choices. Here are some significant thoughts on Discipline 4: Scorekeeping.

2. Measurement Matters: Scorekeeping relies on measuring. It entails quantifying many components of your objective or endeavor. This might contain financial measures, critical performance indicators, or even personal accomplishments.

Without adequate measurement, it's hard to judge development correctly.

3. Clarity and openness: Effective scorekeeping depends on clarity and openness. It's vital to specify what you're measuring and how you're doing it. Everyone engaged should understand the measures and their importance. Transparency creates trust and accountability.

4. Regular Updates: Scorekeeping is not a one-time task. It needs continuous upgrades and monitoring. Regularly collecting and evaluating ratings assist in uncovering patterns and areas that need

improvement. It helps you to make timely modifications to remain on target.

5. Data-Driven choices: When you keep a scorecard, choices become data-driven rather than relying on assumptions or intuition. This data helps you to make educated decisions, manage resources efficiently, and focus efforts where they will have the most significant impact.

6. Motivation and Accountability: Scorekeeping may be a great motivator. It gives a clear picture of progress, which may increase morale and motivate people or teams to reach their goals. Furthermore, it makes people responsible for their performance.

7. Balanced measures: It's crucial to have a balanced collection of measures. Overemphasizing one component while overlooking others might lead to unbalanced priorities. A well-rounded scorecard evaluates many factors of achievement to ensure a comprehensive assessment.

8. constant Improvement: One of the key aims of scorekeeping is to promote constant improvement. By recognizing strengths and shortcomings via data, you may adjust plans and methods, enabling growth and development.

9. Adaptation and Flexibility: While scorekeeping gives an organized strategy,

it's crucial to stay adaptable. Circumstances may change, and so can your measurements and objectives if required. Adaptation is crucial to remaining relevant and successful

# CHAPTER 6:

## OVERCOMING COMMON OBSTACLES

In life, we frequently confront hurdles that might test our growth and perseverance. These impediments might take different forms, from personal disappointments to professional challenges. However, it's crucial to realize that barriers are a natural part of the road towards our objectives. Here are some ideas to assist you in overcoming typical obstacles:

Positive Mindset: Maintain an optimistic mindset. Believe in your ability and concentrate on solutions rather than concentrating on the difficulties.

Goal Clarity: Identify your objectives and priorities. Having a firm sense of purpose will lead you through challenging circumstances.

Resilience: Understand that setbacks are chances for progress. Build resilience by learning from your setbacks and rebounding back stronger.

Seek Support: Don't be hesitant to seek support. Reach out to friends, relatives, or mentors who can give direction and emotional support.

Adaptability: Be open to change. Often, flexibility in your approach might help you identify new, more successful answers.

Time Management: Manage your time efficiently. Prioritize projects and build an organized timetable to approach obstacles methodically.

Continuous Learning: Stay interested and open to learning. Acquiring new skills and information may prepare you to confront problems more effectively.

Stay Persistent: Persistence is crucial to overcome hurdles. Keep moving on, even when the going becomes rough.

Stay Healthy: Take care of your physical and mental well-being. A healthy body and mind are better able to manage problems.

Celebrate Small Wins: Acknowledge and celebrate your victories along the road. Small triumphs may enhance your motivation.

Remember, everyone confronts hurdles at some time. What sets successful people distinct is their capacity to adapt and endure. Embrace these tactics, and you'll find yourself more able to tackle typical difficulties on your route toward success.

- **PROCRASTINATION AND TIME MANAGEMENT**

I hope this note finds you well. I wanted to share some thoughts on the topic of procrastination and time management, as I believe it's a crucial aspect of personal and professional success.

Procrastination is a common habit that can hinder our productivity and overall well-being. It often stems from a lack of motivation, fear of failure, or feeling overwhelmed. However, by practicing effective time management techniques, we can overcome this tendency and make the most of our time.

Here are a few key points to consider:

1. Set Clear Goals: Start by defining your goals, both short-term and long-term. Having a clear sense of what you want to achieve can provide the motivation needed to stay on track.

2. Prioritize Tasks: Not all tasks are created equal. Use methods like the Eisenhower Matrix to distinguish between urgent and important tasks, ensuring that you focus on what truly matters.

3. Create a Schedule: Develop a daily or weekly schedule that allocates specific time slots for various tasks. Stick to this schedule as closely as possible to build a productive routine.

4. Break Tasks into Smaller Steps: Large projects can be overwhelming. Break them down into smaller, manageable tasks to make progress more achievable and less daunting.

5. Minimize Distractions: Identify common distractions and take steps to minimize them. This may involve turning off notifications, finding a quiet workspace, or using website blockers.

6. Use Time Management Tools: There are numerous apps and tools available to help with time management, such as task managers, calendars, and time-tracking apps. Experiment with these to find what works best for you.

7. Reward Yourself: Positive reinforcement can be a powerful motivator. Reward yourself when you accomplish tasks or meet milestones to maintain your enthusiasm.

8. Learn to Say No: Sometimes, overcommitting leads to procrastination. Be selective about the tasks and projects you take on to avoid spreading yourself too thin.

9. Reflect and Adjust: Regularly assess your time management strategies. What's working well? What needs improvement? Adjust your approach as needed to maximize efficiency.

Remember that overcoming procrastination and mastering time management is an ongoing process. It requires self-awareness, discipline, and a commitment to continuous improvement. By implementing these principles, you can take control of your time and achieve your goals more effectively.

- **STAYING FOCUSED AND AVOIDING DISTRACTIONS**

In our fast-paced environment, remaining focused might be a problem, but it's vital for productivity and reaching your objectives. Here are some strategies to help you keep on target and avoid distractions:

Set Clear Goals: Start with a clear idea of what you want to achieve. Having defined objectives in mind can help you keep focused on what's vital.

Prioritize Tasks: Not all chores are equally essential. Identify your most vital duties and handle them first. This decreases the likelihood of becoming diverted by less vital pursuits.

Create a Distraction-Free Environment: Minimize distractions in your workplace. Turn off alerts on your devices, eliminate unneeded tabs, and keep your workplace uncluttered.

Time Management: Use strategies like the Pomodoro method to work in concentrated periods with brief breaks. This might boost your attention and avoid burnout.

Use Technology Wisely: While technology may be a source of distraction, it can also be a beneficial tool. Use programs and solutions intended to help you remain on track, such as productivity apps or website blocks.

Mindfulness and Meditation: Practicing mindfulness and meditation may increase your capacity to be present and prevent wandering thoughts that lead to distractions.

Set Boundaries: Let people know when you require concentrated work time. Establish boundaries with coworkers, friends, and family to limit distractions.

Take Care of Yourself: Ensure you're getting enough sleep, eating healthily, and being active. Physical and mental well-being play a crucial part in your capacity to remain focused.

Break Tasks into Smaller Steps: Complex jobs might be intimidating. Break things down into smaller, attainable stages to make them less frightening and simpler to concentrate on.

Reflect and Adjust: Periodically assess your work habits and determine what distracts you the most. Adjust your techniques properly to consistently enhance your attention.

Remember, keeping focused is a talent that can be mastered over time with practice. By applying these tactics, you'll be better prepared to remain on track, enhance your productivity, and accomplish your objectives.

- **DEALING WITH SETBACKS AND ADVERSITY**

1. I wanted to offer my insights on coping with failures and hardship. Life frequently throws problems our way, and how we react to them may make all the difference. Here are a few crucial considerations to bear in mind:

2. Resilience: Remember that setbacks are a normal part of life. Building resilience is key. Try to regard setbacks as chances for personal development and learning.

3. optimistic Mindset: Maintain an optimistic perspective. Believe in your abilities to overcome problems. A positive outlook may be a great weapon in fighting hardship.

4. Adaptability: Be flexible in your approach. Sometimes, setbacks prompt us to rethink our plans or adapt our ambitions. Adaptability is crucial to going ahead.

5. Support System: Lean on your support network - friends, family, mentors.

Sharing your concerns and seeking advice or encouragement might give important aid.

6. Self-Compassion: Be gentle to yourself. Don't blame yourself for setbacks. Treat yourself with the same kindness you'd show a friend experiencing a similar predicament.

7. Problem Solving: Analyze the setback and find alternative solutions. A proactive strategy might help you restore control and move ahead.

8. Learn from Setbacks: Every setback includes lessons. Take time to think about what went wrong and what you can learn from the experience.

9. Stay Persistent: Perseverance is frequently the key to success. Keep going ahead, even when it seems difficult. Success may be just around the corner.

10. Time Heals: Remember that time may be a tremendous healer. Many setbacks seem less serious as time passes. Keep pushing ahead, even if it's one tiny step at a time.

11. Seek Professional Help: If a setback is causing substantial mental anguish, don't hesitate to seek assistance from a therapist or counselor.

# CHAPTER 7:

## BUILDING ACCOUNTABILITY

Accountability is a cornerstone of personal and professional progress. It's the basis upon which trust, responsibility, and dependability are created. Here are some crucial elements to consider when it comes to developing accountability:

Clear Expectations: Ensure that roles, responsibilities, and objectives are well-defined. When everyone understands what is expected of them, it becomes simpler to hold people responsible for their behavior.

Lead by Example: Leaders have a critical role in establishing the tone for accountability. When leaders are responsible, they establish a standard for the whole team or company to follow.

Open Communication: Foster a climate where team members may freely share successes, problems, and failures. Encourage frequent check-ins to keep everyone informed and aligned.

Establish Metrics: Use quantifiable metrics and key performance indicators (KPIs) to measure success. This gives visible proof of responsibility and enables modifications as required.

Feedback and Recognition: Provide constructive feedback when objectives are fulfilled or missed.

Recognize and reward responsibility to encourage the behavior.

Consequences: While positive reinforcement is necessary, it's equally crucial to address the lack of responsibility. Consistent repercussions for not meeting expectations sustain the integrity of accountability systems.

Ownership: Encourage folks to take ownership of their work. When individuals experience a feeling of ownership, they are more inclined to be responsible for their actions and consequences.

Continuous Improvement: Accountability is not static; it's a continual process. Continuously analyze and develop accountability systems to adapt to changing conditions and aims.

Training and Development: Invest in training and development programs that assist people to enhance their skills and expertise. This may boost their capacity to exceed expectations.

culture change: Building accountability frequently needs a culture change inside an organization. It's not only about policies but about establishing a mentality of accountability and honesty.

Remember that developing accountability is not a one-time effort but a continuous commitment. It's about establishing a culture where employees take responsibility for their activities and strive for excellence, leading to personal and organizational success.

- **CREATING A CULTURE OF ACCOUNTABILITY**

Creating a culture of responsibility is vital for any organization's success. Accountability encourages trust, transparency, and accountability among team members, leading to greater performance and results.

Key measures to build this culture include:

Clear Expectations: Define roles, responsibilities, and objectives for every team member. Ensure everyone knows what's expected of them.

Lead by Example: Leaders should exhibit responsibility in their behaviors and judgments. When leaders accept responsibility, it sets the tone for the whole company.

Effective Communication: Encourage open and honest communication. Team members should feel comfortable sharing obstacles, errors, and progress.

Feedback and Recognition: Provide frequent feedback on performance, recognize accomplishments, and identify areas for improvement.

Consequences for Non-Accountability: Implement equitable repercussions for failing to fulfill promises. This underscores the necessity of responsibility.

Training and Development: Invest in training and development programs to expand skills and knowledge, making it simpler for personnel to perform their duties.

Measurement and Reporting: Establish metrics to evaluate success and hold people and teams responsible. Share outcomes honestly.

Problem-Solving: Encourage problem-solving rather than blaming. When challenges develop, concentrate on finding solutions and avoiding recurrence.

Celebrate Successes: Celebrate triumphs and milestones to increase morale and motivation.

Continued Improvement: Cultivate an attitude of continual improvement. Encourage staff to explore better methods of doing things.

By developing a culture of accountability, companies may better their performance, adjust to difficulties more efficiently, and ultimately accomplish their objectives with a motivated and accountable staff.

- **THE ROLE OF PARTNERS AND TEAMS**

Partnerships and teams play a key part in attaining success throughout different facets of life, from corporate enterprises to personal undertakings. They bring together varied talents, viewpoints, and resources, improving the potential for creativity and advancement. Here are some critical elements to ponder regarding the vital function of partners and teams:

Synergy and

- Collaboration: Partnerships and teams allow people to combine their abilities and experience. When individuals with various skill sets cooperate, they may do more collectively than they might alone. Synergy emerges when each individual adds their unique strengths, leading to new ideas and superior results.

- varied Perspectives: Teams frequently comprise people with varied backgrounds, experiences, and opinions. This variety stimulates creativity and assists in exploring a larger range of alternatives and solutions. It may lead to more well-rounded decision-making and problem-solving.

- Shared accountability: Partnerships and teams foster

shared accountability. Each member is responsible for their unique position and contributes to the overall success of the group. This common commitment helps divide the task and lessen individual stress.

- Risk Mitigation: In business, partnerships may help divide financial risks and obligations. Partners share both earnings and losses, which may offer a safety net during hard times. Likewise, in teams, members help one another, lessening the weight of failure and improving the possibilities of success.

- Learning and development: Working in partnerships and teams frequently gives possibilities for personal and professional development. Individuals may learn from one another, develop new abilities, and widen their minds via exposure to diverse ideas and experiences.

- Efficiency and Productivity: Teams may execute things more efficiently than individuals operating in isolation. The division of labor, better communication, and simplified procedures may contribute to higher productivity and speedier project completion.

- Innovation and Adaptation: Partnerships and teams are well-suited for solving difficult issues and encouraging innovation. When confronted with shifting conditions, teams can adjust and pivot more successfully owing to their combined brainpower and resources.

- Networking: Partnerships may broaden one's network and provide doors to new possibilities. Collaborating with others opens people to a greater variety of connections, which may be helpful in both personal and professional situations.

# CHAPTER 8:

TRACKING AND ANALYTICS

I wanted to stress the relevance of monitoring and analytics in our company operations. In today's data-driven environment, these technologies are important for making educated choices and improving our strategy.

Tracking helps us to track the success of numerous parts of our organization, from website traffic and social media involvement to sales and customer behavior. This data helps us identify what's working and what needs improvement.

Analytics, on the other hand, entails the in-depth study of this data. It reveals trends, patterns, and insights that may drive our decision-making process. For instance, by evaluating consumer data, we may customize our marketing activities and increase client experiences.

- **SETTING UP EFFECTIVE METRICS**

1. Effective metrics serve a significant role in monitoring progress, making informed choices, and attaining success in numerous undertakings, from commercial to personal aspirations. Here are crucial methods to set up and use analytics effectively:

2. Define Clear Objectives: Start by clearly outlining your aims and objectives. What do you wish to achieve? Be precise, quantifiable, and time-bound. Without defined goals, it's tough to determine the correct measurements.

3. Select Relevant Metrics: Choose measurements that closely correlate with your aims. Avoid the desire to measure everything; concentrate on what genuinely matters. For example, in a corporate environment, if you aim to grow revenue, measures like client acquisition cost and monthly recurring revenue are significant.

4. Establish Baselines: Before making modifications or enhancements, establish baseline measurements. This gives a point of comparison to assess progress. It's crucial to know where you began to assess the efficacy of your efforts.

5. Ensure Data Accuracy: Reliable data is vital. Implement data-gathering

techniques and technologies that reduce mistakes and biases. Regularly audit and evaluate your data sources to preserve accuracy.

6. Set objectives and Benchmarks: Define precise objectives or benchmarks for each statistic. These should be ambitious but feasible. Targets give motivation and a clear feeling of progress.

7. Monitor Consistently: Continuously monitor your stats throughout time. Establish a regular reporting plan to be updated about changes and trends. Real-time monitoring may be important for some crucial parameters.

8. Analyze and Interpret: Metrics alone are simply numbers. Interpret the data to understand what it means. Look for relationships, trends, and anomalies. Identify elements that impact the metrics.

9. Adjust Strategies: Metrics should influence your decision-making process. If the data reveals that you're not going toward your objectives, be prepared to modify your strategy and techniques appropriately.

10.Communicate outcomes: Share the outcomes and insights from your metrics with key stakeholders. Effective communication ensures that everyone is aligned and can participate in accomplishing the goals.

11. Iterate and Improve: Metrics are not fixed in stone. As conditions change, so should your metrics. Regularly examine and update your measuring system to be current and effective.

12. Avoid Vanity Metrics: Be aware of indicators that appear good but don't deliver important insights or contribute to your aims. Focus on measurements that motivate action and decision-making.

13. Learn from Failure: Sometimes, measurements may not reach your expectations. Failure may be a useful

learning experience. Analyze what went wrong, adapt your strategy, and go on.

- **ANALYZING YOUR PERFORMANCE**

Taking the time to examine your performance may be a valuable tool for personal and professional progress. Whether you're analyzing your career, your ambitions, or your life in general, this method may help you make educated choices and continual improvements.

Here are some steps to take while reviewing your performance:

Set Clear Objectives: Begin by establishing your objectives and expectations. What do you wish to achieve? Having specific goals will provide you with a baseline to gauge against.

Gather Data: Collect appropriate data and information. This might be work-related measurements, input from others, or personal observations. The more data you have, the better your analysis will be.

Identify Strengths and Weaknesses: Determine what you shine at and where you need improvement. Recognizing your talents may enhance confidence while recognizing faults is vital for progress.

Seek comments: Don't hesitate to seek comments from coworkers, mentors, or friends. They may give useful viewpoints and helpful feedback.

Compare Against Objectives: Evaluate your performance against the objectives you established originally. Are you on track, or do you need to change your approach?

Learn from Mistakes: Mistakes are chances for learning. Analyze what went wrong, why it occurred, and how you may avoid such difficulties in the future.

Celebrate Achievements: Acknowledge and appreciate your victories, no matter how minor. Positive praise might drive you to keep developing.

Make a Plan: Based on your findings, establish a strategy for improvement. Set actionable actions and dates to attain your goals.

Monitor Progress: Regularly monitor your progress versus your strategy. This helps you remain on track and make required modifications as you go.

Reflect and modify: Continuously reflect on your performance and modify your strategy as required. Growth is a constant process.

Remember that examining your performance is not about self-criticism but rather a means to empower yourself with information. It's a useful tool for attaining your objectives and being the best version of your

# CHAPTER 9:

## ADJUSTING YOUR COURSE

Life is a journey filled with unforeseen twists and turns. Sometimes, the route we start on doesn't bring us precisely where we had intended. In these instances, it's vital to recognize the necessity of altering your route.

Just like a ship at sea, we may need to shift our path to sail through storms or take advantage of favorable breezes. It's a sign of knowledge and resilience to realize when the existing route isn't bringing us toward our objectives and to be ready to make the required modifications.

Here are a few crucial considerations to consider while modifying your course:

Self-Reflection: Take time to focus on your present circumstances and your long-term ambitions. Are you still on track? Have conditions changed? Self-awareness is the first step towards making successful improvements.

Flexibility: Be open to change. Embrace the thought that your initial strategy may require revision. Flexibility permits you to adjust to new chances and obstacles.

Learn and Grow: Adjusting your trajectory typically requires learning new skills, obtaining new insights, and collecting fresh information. Don't be hesitant to invest in your personal and professional growth.

Stay tenacious: While altering your path is necessary, it's critical to stay tenacious in the pursuit of your ambitions. Setbacks are part of the road, but persistence may help you overcome them.

Seek help: Don't hesitate to seek guidance and help from trustworthy friends, mentors, or professionals. Sometimes, an outsider's viewpoint may bring significant insights.

Remember, it's not about how many times you modify your path; it's about being dedicated to your final objective. Life's twists and turns may lead to unexpected and stunning discoveries, making the trip itself as significant as the goal.

Embrace change, remain focused on your objectives, and keep altering your path as required. Your path is uniquely yours, and every modification puts you closer to the life you imagine.

- **IDENTIFYING EARLY WARNING SIGNS**

In life, it's frequently stated that prevention is better than cure. This notion holds ppin several dimensions, including personal well-being, relationships, and business. Identifying early warning indicators may make a major difference in preventing possible difficulties and ensuring easier trips.

Early warning indications operate as beacons, highlighting the need for attention and action. Here are some significant places where identifying these indications is crucial:

Health: Paying attention to small changes in your body, such as unexpected aches, weariness, or changes in appetite, might help you discover health problems before they become big ones.

Relationships: In interpersonal relationships, recognizing alterations in communication patterns, increasing stress, or diminished closeness might be early symptoms of danger. Addressing these concerns early may avert more major confrontations.

Finance: Keeping an eye on financial affairs is crucial. Overspending, increasing debt, or erratic income might act as early signals, leading you to examine your financial habits.

Business: In the business sector, identifying market trends, client feedback, or changes in staff morale may help firms adapt and survive in ever-evolving conditions.

Environment: Being attentive to the environment is vital for disaster preparation. Monitoring weather predictions and geological changes may help lessen the effects of natural catastrophes.

Technology: In the digital era, cybersecurity concerns are common. Recognizing odd network activity or questionable communications helps avert data breaches or assaults.

Mental Health: Self-awareness is crucial for mental health. Identifying signs of stress, anxiety, or depression early on may lead to prompt treatments and enhanced emotional well-being.

Remember, detecting early warning indicators isn't about forecasting every conceivable issue but rather creating a proactive mentality. It's about being watchful, adaptive, and prepared to take action when required. By doing so, you empower yourself to manage life's problems with more resilience.

- **MAKING MID-COURSE CORRECTIONS**

Recognizing successes is vital for various reasons. Firstly, it promotes motivation and morale. When people get credit for their successes, it validates their efforts and inspires them to strive for perfection. Secondly, acknowledgment encourages a pleasant work or social atmosphere. It promotes a culture of gratitude and collaboration, where people encourage one another's achievement. Additionally, praising successes may assist in identifying top performers, which can be important for promotions and career growth. Overall, acknowledging successes not only honors individual triumphs but also adds to personal progress and community prosperity.

# CHAPTER 10 :

## THE IMPORTANCE OF RECOGNIZING ACHIEVEMENTS

Recognizing successes is vital for various reasons. Firstly, it promotes motivation and morale. When people get credit for their successes, it validates their efforts and inspires them to strive for perfection. Secondly, acknowledgement encourages a pleasant work or social atmosphere. It promotes a culture of gratitude and collaboration, where people encourage one other's achievement. Additionally, praising successes may assist identify top performers, which can be important for promotions and career growth. Overall, acknowledging successes not only honors individual triumphs but also adds to personal progress and community prosperity.

## • MOTIVATION THROUGH SUCCESS

Success is a tremendous motivator, motivating people to attain higher heights and accomplish their objectives. When we experience success, whether great or little, it produces a positive feedback loop that drives our motivation.

Success brings a feeling of success and affirmation for our efforts. It reminds us that our hard work and commitment may lead to concrete rewards. This, in turn, enhances our confidence and self-belief, making us more motivated to take on new tasks.

Moreover, success acts as a guide for future initiatives. It tells us that having objectives, developing a strategy, and persisting may lead to beneficial results. When we reflect on our prior victories, we receive the motivation and resolve required to overcome challenges and strive for even greater achievements.

In essence, success is not only a destination but a continuing source of drive. It keeps us focused, determined, and ready to follow our ambitions. So, embrace your victories, no matter how tiny they may appear, and let them push you into a future filled with even more extraordinary achievements.

# CHAPTER 11

: BEYOND THE 12-WEEK YEAR

1. I wanted to share my ideas with you on the concept of moving "Beyond the 12-week Year." While the 12-week Year is a strong framework for attaining objectives, it's crucial to remember that personal and professional progress doesn't end there.

2. The 12-week Year pushes us to split our long-term objectives into shorter, more achievable portions, which is helpful. However, it's vital to regard this as simply

one step in our road towards achievement. Here's why:

3. Continuous Growth: Achieving a single 12-week objective is a tremendous achievement, but it shouldn't be the end of your desire. Continuously creating and working towards new objectives is vital for continuous progress.

4. Adaptability: Life is unpredictable, and occasionally circumstances change. Going beyond the 12-week year requires being adaptive and altering your objectives as required to remain on the correct track.

5. Lifelong Learning: The pursuit of knowledge and skill improvement should

be continual. Make it a habit to study, develop, and remain relevant in your area.

6. Balanced Life: Success is not simply about professional success. Consider your personal life and well-being as part of your long-term ambitions. Balance is vital to happiness and contentment.

7. Legacy Building: Think about the legacy you wish to leave behind. Going beyond the 12-week year enables you to concentrate on projects and activities that have a lasting effect.

- **INTEGRATING THE 12-WEEK YEAR INTO YOUR LONG-TERM PLANS**

In our pursuit of personal and professional growth, it's essential to strike a balance between short-term achievements and long-term aspirations. One effective strategy to bridge this gap is by integrating the concept of the "12-Week Year" into our long-term plans.

The 12-week Year is a productivity framework that condenses a traditional year into shorter, highly focused 12-week cycles. This approach is designed to enhance accountability, urgency, and results. Here's how you can seamlessly weave it into your long-term plans:

1. Define Clear Objectives: Start by articulating your long-term goals and aspirations. These might include career milestones, personal development, or

financial targets. Ensure they are Specific, Measurable, Achievable, Relevant, and Time-bound (SMART).

2. Break Down into 12-Week Segments: Once your long-term goals are established, break them down into smaller, manageable objectives that can be accomplished within a 12-week timeframe. This step ensures that you maintain focus on your overarching goals while making consistent progress.

3. Set Quarterly Goals: Each 12-week cycle becomes a "quarter" in your long-term plan. Set specific goals for each quarter that align with your overall objectives.

These shorter deadlines create a sense of urgency and commitment.

4. Plan Strategically: Develop detailed plans for each 12 weeks. Identify the key actions, milestones, and tasks needed to achieve your quarterly goals. Make sure your plans are flexible enough to adapt to changing circumstances.

5. Regular Review and Adjustments: Consistently review your progress at the end of each 12-week cycle. Celebrate your achievements and learn from your setbacks. Adjust your long-term plans and quarterly goals based on your experiences and evolving priorities.

6. Stay Accountable: Share your goals and progress with a mentor, coach, or accountability partner. Their support and feedback can be invaluable in maintaining your commitment to the 12-week Year approach.

7. Balance Short-Term Wins and Long-Term Vision: Remember that while the 12-week Year focuses on short-term results, it should always serve your long-term vision. Ensure that the quarterly goals you set align with your ultimate objectives.

By integrating the 12-week Year into your long-term plans, you create a dynamic and adaptive framework for achieving your dreams. This approach fosters a sense of accomplishment every 12 weeks, propelling you towards your overarching goals with renewed energy and focus.

Stay committed, stay adaptable, and watch as your long-term aspirations become a series of successful 12-week sprints

## ● EVOLVING YOUR GOALS AND VISION

I wanted to offer my views on the necessity of updating our objectives and vision. In life, change is inevitable, and so should our objectives. As we grow, learn, and adapt, our objectives should too. Here are a few crucial items to consider:

Embrace Change: The world around us is continuously shifting, and our objectives should reflect that. Don't be hesitant to alter your vision to suit your changing interests, beliefs, and circumstances.

Continuous Learning: As you study and obtain new talents, your objectives might grow more ambitious. Embracing lifelong learning may offer new chances and extend your outlook.

Flexibility: Being dogmatic in your aims might lead to frustration. Be open to pivoting when required, and remember that diversions may occasionally lead to unexpected and great destinations.

Reevaluate Regularly: Set aside time occasionally to examine your objectives and vision. Are they still relevant to you? Do they match with your existing priorities? Adjust as required.

Seek Inspiration: Look to mentors, role models, and various experiences for inspiration. They may help you develop your vision and give vital insights.

Short-term vs. Long-term: Balance short-term aims with long-term vision. Short-term objectives give direction and drive, while the long-term vision keeps you focused on the greater picture.

Celebrate Milestones: Acknowledge and appreciate your victories along the road. This may feed your motivation and create a feeling of satisfaction.

Remember, updating your objectives and vision is a natural aspect of personal development. It's a reflection of your versatility and readiness to welcome new chances. So, be open, keep learning, and keep aiming for a future that thrills and delights you.

# Conclusion

Life is a journey filled with possibilities and difficulties, and how we handle it may make all the difference. One strong thought that might revolutionize the way we live our lives is the idea of enjoying a lifetime of 12-week years.

In a world where time appears to slip through our fingers, the 12-week year concept encourages us to split our long-term objectives into shorter, more achievable intervals. Instead of waiting for the typical calendar year to create and accomplish objectives, we break our aspirations into 12-week portions.

Why is this so effective? First, it produces a feeling of urgency. Knowing that we only have 12 weeks to achieve meaningful change encourages us to prioritize and concentrate on what is genuinely important. It avoids the procrastination and complacency that frequently come with long-term objectives.

Second, the 12-week year method fosters consistent activity. By defining quarterly objectives, we create a habit of frequent review and revision. We're more likely to keep responsible for our targets, monitor our success, and change our plans as required.

Furthermore, it lowers the overwhelm associated with huge, far-off ambitions. Breaking things into tiny, manageable goals makes them less scary and more feasible. This thinking adjustment may lead to a more satisfying and productive existence.

So, when you begin on your adventure, consider enjoying a lifetime of 12-week years. Whether it's personal improvement, job goals, or any other effort, this technique may help you make continuous progress, retain concentration, and finally realize your objectives.

Here's to a lifetime of meaningful, 12-week travels filled with development and success

9 798863 208299